RAW GOODS INVENTORY

T0108909

Winner of the Iowa Poetry Prize

Raw Goods

Inventory

EMILY ROSKO

University of Iowa Press   IOWA CITY

University of Iowa Press, Iowa City 52242
Copyright © 2006 by Emily Rosko
http://www.uiowa.edu/uiowapress
All rights reserved
Printed in the United States of America
Design by Richard Hendel

No part of this book may be reproduced or used
in any form or by any means without permission
in writing from the publisher. All reasonable steps
have been taken to contact copyright holders of
material used in this book. The publisher would
be pleased to make suitable arrangements with
any whom it has not been possible to reach. This
is a work of poetry; any resemblance to actual
events or persons is entirely coincidental.

The University of Iowa Press is a member of
Green Press Initiative and is committed to
preserving natural resources.

Printed on acid-free paper

Library of Congress Cataloging-in-Publication Data
Rosko, Emily, 1979–.
Raw goods inventory / by Emily Rosko.
    p.   cm.—(The Iowa poetry prize)
ISBN 0-87745-980-0 (pbk.)
I. Title.   II. Series.
PS3618.084425R39 2006
811'.6—dc22   2005053862

06   07   08   09   10   P   5   4   3   2   1

For my parents,

my sister,

and for Anton—who fixes things.

CONTENTS

ACKNOWLEDGMENTS

Thank you to the editors of the publications where the following poems first appeared, some in earlier versions: the *American Poetry Journal*: "Wave Factor" and "Bundle"; *Another Chicago Magazine*: "Ventriloquized Bodies" and "Measures"; the *Beloit Poetry Journal*: "Raw Goods Inventory"; *Borderlands: Texas Poetry Review*: "Pigskin"; *Cimarron Review*: "Resort"; *Columbia: Journal of Literature and Art*: "A Sorry Concept, That Town"; the *Denver Quarterly*: "Tongues of" and "The Toy Divine(s)"; *DIAGRAM*: "Conduct"; the *Florida Review*: "In the Land of Sleeping People"; *Hubbub*: "Pall"; *In Posse Review*: "Aquatic" and "What's Discovered is Wiped Out"; *Meridian*: "Dzien Dobry"; the *National Poetry Review*: "Hot Air," "Elephant," and "Glossitic"; the *Notre Dame Review*: "Entry" and "Slip" (as "Scrap"); *Octopus*: "Insulation" and "Less Art, More Monkeys"; *Pleiades*: "Clockwork"; *Quarterly West*: "Even before Your Elbow Knocked Over the Glass"; the *Sow's Ear Poetry Review*: "What Closes" and "Lives of Astrologers"; *Sycamore Review*: "At the Sushi Arcade"; *Tar River Poetry*: "Sleeping Bear Dunes"; *Tarpaulin Sky*: "Clearing the Yard" and "Blind Feel"; and the *Yalobusha Review*: "Before Surgery." "Even before Your Elbow Knocked Over the Glass" was featured on Verse Daily (www.versedaily.org), March 8, 2003. "Elephant" appeared on Verse Daily, December 20, 2004.

For their generosity and support, my gratitude goes to the Jacob K. Javits and the Ruth Lilly Fellowship Programs, the Dorothy Sargent Rosenberg Memorial Fund; to Cornell University's Creative Writing Program and Stanford University's Stegner Fellowship Program. Thank you to Matthew Hittinger and Sarah Masengarb for their encouragement and friendship.

Detritus. Because truth accrues in

pieces. As in Elise saying, "You're a stinko,"
then becoming a pink streak

in the grass. I couldn't handle such guiltless

honesty, the smile would do
me in. I'm in for the payoff, the pileup

of vulnerabilities turned fruit, no more

cuttings left to mold in glass vases, one
less jack to join the file share. *Everything ends,*

everything comes out even; a line—and a sum

total. It's enough to be a box
within oneself, to have a fence

barbwired and electrified, wholly

treed. Because an open gate is loss
of privacy, I'm keeping tight-

bolted, debuting in full fig.

If I think of any beginning I think water
down to the taproot, cell base, underground

aquifers that stretch Nebraska's ends: the stillness
of the lake mornings and vapor pocketed

in the grazing fields. Clouds
releasing the first skeptical drops, next sheets

to overfill land: torrents, then torrents
not for years. The sea's upwelling cold gone

warm: migration, source-seeking, the murder a full well
could draw. On the prairie runoff frets

the rock, the tributaries chemical-rich
deposit silt: dead zone in the Gulf

of Mexico. All's glassy, gold-
glinted from above: pond, chlorine

blue pools. Iced Pluto knows no liquid: no mineral
congregate or cave formation. Snow-

still, hushed as it was here before: glacier
in retrograde, the moraines seeded and greened.

Adaptation among organisms: salt to fresh to
in between. Uptake in the xylem, circulation

in the vein: miracle, madness, exit: water
as a means, shaped by its container,

formless so that each formed thing
takes mass—waterlogged, exposed.

To say it was over and done with no harm
wasn't really the case. The hemlocks wind-

burnt, losing. Fishermen wrestle with, hook salmon
in high lead content water. Stunned look, the red

frayed marks. It's better: eyes averted, both
of us tucked in, knees touching. Placement,

the stars rocking in their cradles. Always:
the dream of the dog alive again. Such childish

dreams, such disregard for the stock market. He
was kind enough to leave the proper notes, one

to each child, and to phone the police
ahead of time. Oblivious cow in a nearby

field, emulating nothing but cowness. Shoulder-
propped, spring-loaded. So easy to use no wonder

it's number one. Oh clocked moon, calibrate
our hearts! The boy inflamed and not taking

no for an answer. Lord, give strength. Sympathies:
the windy sky parts now in flocks. All the I'm-so-sorry-

for-your-loss and help-me-help-you's. Then a starling
took to nesting in the chimney. Not a gift or a treasure

hidden, long searched-for. The sun just a penny
as it slips through pockets of cloud. Houses locked in

shadow. A round of quarter moons left till winter
solstice. I won't tell you again how

it happened—the quick leaving, the sound a splinter
through ice. You've got it wrong, sleepyhead, it's

snow sheeting in across the lake. No
miracle, just water congregating around dust.

Nights, the moon patrolled the sky. The whole valley
lidded in a haze trees don't overgrow
but thicken in. You: a sad thing in the middle. The roses
spotted and yellowing. So a little devastation
happens—fungus, voles, lack of this or that. Hills
quilted with soy and corn add no quaintness
to the palsied farmhouses, the highway shoved next
to them. Nor do the rocks winter-sky shaded stacked
human-head size for barn walls preserve the picture:
cement brittling, the keystone centered by collapse, and you
down in the scrub pines, all tinder and hush.

And then a valve tightened inside her—

She said, *if only* and *what if*
turning it over

until *deserve* became exclusive, low-
spoken, drawn back in the throat.

Sanctuary, said the house, but it wasn't—

the roof chronically leaking, carpenter
ants circling the sink.

Mornings, fear became the container
that kept her. She thought *this*

can go that can go next. And it went—

Repose, said the roses
after they opened, but she couldn't.

The curtains pulled. Along
the rainspout, wisteria twined, thick.

That's it, she said. And it was—

Even after folding into herself,
refuse remaining.

Underneath in limbo, there's only the thought of the corpse

resurfacing. Sound down there is

muffled, the ear funnels a higher frequency. The drowned can't

lean over to care, can't take in the surround. Water

is a cushion, the currents girdle the skin,

sanction every pore. Numbers

of bodies ride the transverse motion, legs elevated.

It's a kind of prayer: their whole mass levitating, then

sinking. There's no reparation for what

the lake gives them—muddy

bottom, rain dimpling above, trout

finning through. Permanent static, no summons, no

wish but to breach or settle.

What started out simple
became a force tearing into the middle—
each chord spiraling out.
 Not noise, but a continuous

count and tension. I had to think of scratches
  on tape, zero and one,
language slinking through.
I had to think: this pencil isn't a bow

in my hands. There should be more surface, more
  bone. The instructor said to
imagine the skeletal structure beneath the muscle
  and skin. I fattened the frame, edged

the contours until the body resembled a
  topographic map—the lines'
 wood-grained complexion, the torso
a knotted mass. Under it, the lungs grappled

with full- and emptiness—the space was
unmarked, the husk
 of the instrument varnished, clean.
I coddled the neck, fuddled the fingers, I drew

 it out, smudged the definition.
It couldn't be undone—tangle of music,
movement, the hand
outstripped. Errors without shape—the knees

 that held it, the strings, the sweep
from shoulder to elbow to wrist, fiber
and nerve.
 I didn't erase a thing.

Accuracy is the mark of love
   so I enter from the skew,
   pick apart the ribs. No cadaver
     for the faint-hearted, not
     vulture-clean or under

warranty, this matter accepts the knife
   as Jell-O a spoon. The results:
   hybrids: the pansy
     injected with a new color
     palette of buff yellows,

gray to purple blotches; sunsets
   contained in hydrogen, split
   electrons in glass tubes. Tied
     to prevent seepage, the uterus
     takes the prod, insect-thin

syringe suctioning eggs: plasmic,
   cryopreserved. No more intimate
   than a funeral, no less
     punishing than a little light
     dentistry before lunch. Precision's

in the splice, the genes matched
   and repaired: pig in tomato, human
   protein in rice. A greater yield
     for the me generation: quicker
     maturity, better plastics, newfound

viral strains. Because a good lineage inspires
   confidence, I constellate the compounds,
   apply ego to nature: for baldness,
     rodents. Timely cures, and all
     human errors are impatience.

Poppy-face, database: there's been some
   excessive growth in the bloom
   department. Too much
     correction has made the cart
     tip. Yes, the garden's overrun.

I say *process*, but the brain doesn't
               cooperate. The splendor of it is
      that it can't go on

                    forever, unlike the clock.
              Its miniature gears comb their teeth
                    within each other, turn and feed—

There's something in me ready
               to drop. Hard not to think *flower*, or
     beehive—the poster of the female
           reproductive system, pink

                  and ripe on the doctor's wall.
              Seems shameful, looking in—the organs
        neatly packed give no
          room for—

Sputter in the valve
               and the whole thing stops. The hands at
       quarter past. An electric pulse can kill
         the battery at the moment of

                      release. The soul dilates
               or hemorrhages, it doesn't stay
           enmeshed in the fine
               network of ligament

and folds. The body repairs
             itself to a certain point then
        spills, resets. More

division than cluster
           around the center. Time was
      droplets, shadow-play—
                the brain keeps count.

So much for faith in mechanics, the grease. As long as
the pump keeps chugging and the engine slurs its vowels in
baby talk, then life is good. Forget *awry*—it doesn't fit
in the lexicon. The hysterical has gone comic. Even
then *outburst* meant bitten tongue (keep it in, don't spoil
supper). Put a little elbow into it. All this digging for
China with plastic yellow shovels and no vision
is going to grace us, no word from either ether-world. He's
got passivity shoved in his gullet. She's got beauty in fits,
thinness draping her bones. I could say *steady* all night long.
Add a pinch of love to it. The brain rushes with its crash
and can't get up. The whip of it keeps us panting,
the sting-swell keeps us from asking for more.

A CHAMELEON

you say, as though the skin sack
will give it away. Peel this off
and that. What's left? Some scatter, some air. A green

rush capsizing into blue, a tree wrecked with a tree
disease. Motionless, all stare, its prehensile
tail coiled, stone-patient. Transparent—

no—defense is your mistake, take the drab
for dead. You fill in the slight
adjustments, sort the shadow from the smear

of its exact, furious tongue. Longer
and things get unsorted, a scaled repetition meshed
into leaves. A green, a fuzz of air, tree

disheveled from its tree-ease. For competition, the glare
is weapon, until stress finishes one off. Turncoat
of the pincer-footed, the eye in swivel, the other

in rove. All this fuss for the curious thing
smack front of you: monkish, gravel-fine.
Fickle—no—divine.

Extinguish—the flame pinches,

snakes into smoke, is consumed. A fire
breather has to vaseline her lips so the fluid she
spits into strings of flame doesn't singe

the mouth. That and the sword

swallower, arching back
the neck, steel through the esophagus—
the x-ray broadcasting how the point

rests on stomach's bottom. Not so far-

fetched, this folly a trick
or miracle. St. Teresa of Ávila's heart
pierced—golden heat arrowed in.

Ecstasy—

a fingerprint emblazoned on her
sternum. In this state, it's all one
tongue—tender curl and whip.

Put the holy spirit to flight and you'll find vacancy.
Not so much centered
                              in the chest as lower

down, more withered and less conceived
of. No lady could be spared—

the female left to fit
                              and the visions recorded by a literate

hand. In a pro-male-
                              force economy

only Portuguese mares were deemed more
lustful. The gaze of one

could send a woman to orgasm, influence
the fetus so it came out
                              horsey, hooved.

Uterine fury. Rightness wasn't the topic
                    but how to keep her from her

own fancies—a demon
roaming through,
                    stirring the organs to hysterics, lewd

poses. As penned,
                    women were made for feeling

and feeling meant a brain's
white fever.
                    No nail for the hand. Inarticulate

body. The less of it, the more
spiritualized she becomes.

THE TOY DIVINE(S)

I've had my plastic horses, the arc of their
    belly and veins raised in muzzle, delicately

    tendoned ankles. The malicious gleam of
their eyes, marbles washed from dirt.

                Stones. All those things kept

in jars, shoeboxes, what I'd rub fingers over—
    the polished surface, doeskin hat and feather of the

    marionette with a jacked spine, and splintery
wooden matryoshkas inside, inside one

                another. A voodoo doll—its x'ed

out eyes and mouth, yarn hair and red
    heart signifying where to stick

    the pin. The x equals every and
nix, notta—meaning crossed out, marks the

                spot, signature. Roman numeral ten—

one and zero—the thing becoming what it
    stands for. Perfection like that

    comes in a package, crafted by careful hands of
Southeast Asian women. Someone put the

                (kisses, skull-and-bones, jacks)

pieces together, someone painted its hooves
    black. Tyco, Mattel branded on

the hind, or stuffed and tagged with a prefab
name. *One was so busy keeping you—*

                  invisible pet on a leash—

alive that no one had time to determine what you were.
    Unanswerable thing, you are equalizer,

    pretender, the self-in-question. There's no
formula for your forlornness,

                (the soul = polyester filling)

or mine. *Invisible substance.* Crude representation.
    I've put as much of me in you as

    you could handle. There wasn't much.
I've retired a horse with a busted leg,

                pushed in the pin—

Fumble, and it's half-wit
                barn-hands trying to tackle
            the pig—it slips out from the
belly, can't be handled
                without finesse. The baby

            glossed and not breathing until ankled
upside down and slapped on the ass. A sour-milk
                stink like outdated candy
            from the chocolate shop I worked
at that went to fatten hogs

                in Illinois. They'd shove IVs full
            of corn syrup, Coke—glucose high and I swear
that's what got those athletes fainting
                on the field. As 4-H club kids they bred
            their stock for the State Fair. The girl

across the street produced a two
                hundred pound sow and later one
            of her own. At school, the fetus arrived
in a formaldehyde-filled plastic
                bag. We were to dissect—first the piglet's

            underside through the intestines. Nervous
system by the end of the week, we slit
                along the spine, the skull. Some joker
            sliced from ear to ear, peeled the face
off, pressed it mask-like against his. Porker,

                swine—the thing can scream and will
            when its legs are tied. At the Fair, it's wrestle
a pig and take it home. Rain, and the turf
                becomes slop. There goes Chester,
            Buttercup, weaned from a bottle.

You could fry an egg on it.
                    Records buckle.
          What doesn't wilt expands—

clematis sprouts from twigs and cords
              through lattice. A watchdog is knocked out
in the shade. Clouds congeal over the lake

              harvesting moisture—graying. The elderly
are warned to jack up the A/C while others
              abandon work to sink

into cool sheets.
          Wait it out, we're told—
The earth was once this way—it steamed

for ages then shrank under
          ice. All that is worthwhile lies in mute
places—diamonds pinched between rock and ossified

          remains of animals we learned about
from cartoons. We weren't as fearful of mass
          destruction then—
                    unknown debris in space, or atoms

contained and hurled against each
          other in a cyclotron. There were duck-
and-cover methods, shelters for meltdown,

          mountains to store waste as it
decays, half-lives spent and the notorious
          two-headed monsters created. For entertainment

          the neighborhood kids hit one another
with water balloons. Some blond boys

pair up and pelt an auburn girl—

A radio crackles feverishly. Carpenter
        bees whine in the porch wood.
                        She'll grow a thick skin.

---

skeletal the same week she barred the bedroom door, each night
plugged in her glow-in-the-dark Mary-the-Virgin icon. Electronic
conversion. Call it what you want—she was off-center

in the head. Large numbers and an iron-penny taste
in her mouth. We slept too easily in the wooden-lacquered house
to notice. Humidity made the siding bloat and shrink—hot days, cool

evenings. Cracks filled in with putty so the hornets wouldn't nest. All
the flowers drew them. I took the stinger out myself, cleaned up after
the dog did its duty in the neighbor's yard. She was pissing herself in

bed, would soak the sheets, change, stay wired listening to the buzz of
things. No one mentioned it. I was too young and always
hearing things anyway—the talkings-to I received. Bad attitude,

spunk. Get that outta you. She never took the blame—a fig tree
withered from coldshock by a window left open. It wasn't the faults
we added up, it was the way they didn't matter, how she didn't

register. The many-rayed yellow heads—fields of them.

The way the room felt
with her in it—incomplete,

an epicenter for impulse. Even
number of flowers for a funeral,
odd for other occasions. She took one

look and rearranged the room. Bone
thin she was and resolute
as the lilies upright in glass. Compact, hard-

pressed. The way her leg broke clean in two
places. The way she walked,
the way she walks now—half-

socked, tilted. The sumac
reddening on the hills. Heat-driven,
blade lightning, heartquake—

what pulses through the body dulls
its sting in the ground. It
was no accident. The way bitterness enters—

I could take her in my arms, I could take
her by the arm lead her, I
could take her, lead her through

the doorway. We'd go hand
in hand, we'd pass
through, we'd pass. No

one could touch her. I could—

1: Snow Maiden

The meteoric night is behind you, the moth-speckled
canvas lasts as long as your eyes are closed. Whirling
universe, edged with laser precision. Branches plated
with clinquant—blossom or berry, silver-
sparked. Fuzzy data in the field: digitalized,
planted. Your bundled shoulders and basket
filled with lilies, your one offering. Scarf ice-
caked, wind-roused. Turn into what is
surely cold, stone-quiet. You are just one
minuscule dot, zeroed on your square of snow.

2: Andromeda

The daughter pays for beauty, must
be sacrificed. Reach out your arm. The naked
eye can see your makeup: companion
galaxies, elliptical and certain, take
residence in your body. The chain
that binds you is beyond blood: the program
installed before you were born. A gilded warrior
on wingèd horse who saved you from
oblivion. Or did he? Fixed
in the northern hemisphere between
husband and intemperate mother, others
peer at you, mark every blemish. Fortune-drawn,
charted. You give the faintest wince, blush.

3: Renée Jeanmarie in "La Belle au Bois Dormant"

Limbs extended, your *penche arabesque* is what's holding
off the thicket. Clouded neural mass, atomic
dust storm. In the toes and fingers, balance
rests. Knife-straight, you remain positioned
in the wind that nets your frame. The ceiling
above you folds back, reveals some unknowable
variable—time warp or rip. Nothing else. Space
is shrink-wrapped in itself, closing. In the center,
your confident Y—structure, not question.

What flickers isn't heavenly light, but the discredited
        pen moving across numbers
                with the stealth of a murderer.
Whoever you are, I'm not here

        to answer your call. I've been sidetracked
                by meteor showers, knocked cold by
the flu. I've taken to burying raccoons electrocuted
        along the gated high-security community. Stay away

        from what hums. Stay away from shiny temptations
laid on the table by a dirty hand. Power
        lines thread through the ground, satellites circuit
                and corrupt the zodiac. What bad news

will come on sluggish steps and how long
        should I wait with an extra dollar pinned
                to my underwear? Spend
what you have, grasshopper, and come closer,

        bring me your small flash, whatever instant
                gladness you have to share. I'm not trained
in the martial arts, every part is vulnerable,
        especially the underside of the tongue. I've covered

                every entry in the book, each charted
point condenses to now. It's true
        nothing can be moved without a triggering
                effect. There are no pushers, there is

motion within motion. Why not stay still, stick
        around awhile? Speak to me
                about things if only the weather.
There's humanness in it.

Sometimes I get a terrific headache when I am conversing with
and/or listening to you. For the past ten minutes, I've given
subtle clues—forced yawns and the rattle of car keys. Your
drivel could fuel a bulldozer, it could scare
away a burglar. Maybe I'll escape to
the deserted drive-in lot where the movie screen is missing
panels and is overshadowed by pines. Who cares that no
lights are flickering, no brunette is being wooed
by the rough rider? I'll stay here to get a piece
of mind, to observe nature—the yellow-bellied
finches that flit about in packs. Maybe if we could
retain the moment when we learn to love
who we are, we could get something done, help
the paraplegic paint with his toes or start
a campaign for quiet hours. Congratulations
would be in order for the one
who doesn't speak the longest. I'd cut
the motor. Vehicles have their own chatter, belly-fart
of motorcycles gussied up by reputation—leather
and long hair, shoot-outs in a casino. If we talked more
about the things that matter then these things
wouldn't happen. So I've heard, but you missed
the best line—the part where they're up
close, and she's about to kiss the renegade
goodbye. She says: *Tell me I'm beautiful then put a lid on it.*

—So the brain has
      its ups and down, the body
   follows. Chemical-rushed, fabricated
        or not, each neuron is doused with mood:
  tickle-pink or correct blue. Muscles
      slackened or on
    edge, the response defined
by what floods in (punk-studded, fireworks).

Not a fuzzy feeling lodged
     behind the brain's undoing, nothing can keep
  it from that. Not ice for a center,
       (though you've been called
    that: *icy*) its engine warmth
     corrodes the mechanism,
  loosens the cannon.

Adrenaline, not testosterone, incites it: faulty
     wire, a tip-off that keeps tipping
  back spinally until the whole
      organic thing is lit
   and the staircase up to the loft
     is barricaded. Who said it doesn't burn?
Anger has its drillings: the mined-for comeback,

the staying power of grudge-work. Knucklehead,
    this yarn ball has no start or end.
  I'll cool mine, you yours. There
      are other fits to be had: nutshell,
   abstraction, the gods, fiddle. We should bring
    to standstill this tornadic row, kiss
goodbye this streak of mean.

Mirrored in the screen, my face turns impish,
nose elongated, eyes spread. I'm convincing myself
my profile isn't asymmetrical, it's cultured.
My sister says I could be in a magazine.
As a teenager, she spent nights flipping
through *Cosmo*, indulging in the healthy skin
glow the ads promise. There's no image of beauty

to measure against here. The moon glares
like a store clerk and the rich kids have scored
smack outside. No one gives a squat
whether you have a sister. These punks
just look you up and down, swagger by.
In back, the manager's engrossed in Clive
Barker. On his pinkie, a gold ring he rubs
against his chin, he mouths

the words. Sometimes I can't speak to save
my life. I'm in a slump, my last
quarter eaten by the skee-ball machine.
Sushi aging under neon, fingerprints
on the deli case, crack and ditty
of video games. I'd proposition
that guy glued to Ms. Pacman, if he'd turn
my way, but he's ingesting ghosts, racking

up points. I want someone who makes numbers
do the work for you, earn you a house
on the coast, a cottage in the Poconos.
Sometimes the want is so sharp it leaves me
hooked to electronic solitaire, beat-the-devil,
until I think of my bed as a soft immunity,
the pillow unruffled, and I'm too helpless

to decipher the order. When I shuffle
out of here, my hair is riddled with smoke.
Hustlers punctuate the sidewalk, feet cinched
in high heels, headlights butcher my eyes
and it's not inspirational when the stars unpack
the sky. I'm slipping in the night's
inhibitions, fastening to the names of businesses,
to billboards, to every loophole
of this rigged contest.

Oh, clouds that do not look like cherubs, move over! My heart
isn't big enough to include you. The crows shit on
my car every morning, such

gratuitous little fellows—the things I never asked for. Oh,
   unrecognized
genius, the modest beauty wasting from
illness, the good-kid-turned-bad. Failing

grade, summer heat. Oh, row of desks I loathed sitting at. In
school, we hatched chickens from an incubator, eggs
in rotation, the chicks deformed. One

with thin chest skin and no ribs—the organs sludged
and its cheep-cheep cries. The animals my mother made me
return—the rabbit, the toad, the slug. Oh, child

tossing a ball alone! The dandelions are systematically doused
with chemicals—the chemicals you'll sniff
as a teenager, the brain the unrepining side-kick.

Dear sister whom I cannot relate to, I surrendered my popsicles
to you! Friend who kept my videotapes. Ex-lover,
you fall so clumsily through old poems. Book, you

looked better on the shelf! Oh, the philomaths are paraphrasing
other people's theories, the same drivel! Numbers and words,
teleological trinkets that can't retain the world. Over

a thousand monarchs frost-nipped in Mexico—untranslatable
odor. Oh, sex-drive that won't be active forever! Oh,
old woman I will someday become! Take stock now, I say, use

your flexibility. Stomach stay flat, breasts don't droop any time
soon. Oh, body, you were once small

and resilient—you could shimmy through

tight places. Mind, you were sparked; heart, uninjured. I am
such a thing. Lazy day. Oh, wizened hickory,
I too grow out of myself.

Because it covers you. Because you can't
disrobe the mind's grudges.
                      That wind-tousled sheet,

the hemline breezing the dirt. Ankles, tender-
marked thigh.
                  Mica specks down the sun
for closer inspection. Because no *away*

comes without *from*, and the *from*
is not without its own tangles.

Because I've heard how that goes. The bits
rub off and soak in
                (all buckle-
shine and unscuffed shoes). Because

here's a sorry concept
                (a run in the stockings),
and the *listen to this*'s purpose is
to be heard,
                altered where necessary. Because

it hurt to stand still like that.
                Between looking clean
and upright, between who's the better
son or daughter.
            Line and pin.

Because this cut doesn't suit me.

Clouds rolled in, beach-fat over the valley,
and hunkered down, dropped all they could. Then came
the yellow days

of winter, filled with boredom.
The steel mill's machinery strained under its shrink
and the snow went gray

as it fell. No star-
view, the panorama blotted as the worn-out
hills cupped

the exhaust. We were low-
landed, hemmed in by what provided
for us. Shops closed, and the last

train to Pittsburgh took off
with that name. Icicles clung to the cut-rock
along the highway.

No letting up: the snow then snow-
melt, rain. Upstream was bloated,
a buckle close

to bursting. Faulty dam and
spillway. A buck or two off the cost
for no drain basin.

And there we were, dozing
in crummy houses stacked together,
beneath "surely the day will come."

Yet, those thoughts
comforted, it was the one thing
we could have.

It wasn't the tomatoes in the garden but a cardinal,
dart-red, that grazed our attention. An old Polish
wives' tale says the bird signals someone
is about to die. It's customary not to speak,
but to cover your face from it, let it
fly off on its own. My mother

told me this after the death of her mother.
What hearsay!— there are no cardinals
outside of this continent. It
spooked us anyway, the Polish
have a way of doing that—speaking
in hushed tones in public, as if someone

might hear you blaspheming and someone
always did. For years my grandmother
crossed herself twice a day and spoke
about money as though it were a cardinal
sin. She tried to converse with us in Polish—
dobrze, meaning good, meaning it

is all I can retain. What's *good* for, if it
can't enter your day like someone
you haven't seen for ages, maybe outside a Polish
bakery, where the happily plump owner mothers
you with poppy seed? I can sympathize with the cardinal
unaware of the ill will it brings. When I spoke

with her last, the dill was overshot, in a way of speaking,
and already reseeding. The garden was it
for her—the last peaceful place, until that cardinal
came swooping in from someone
else's backyard feeder. My mother
got a broom, cursed at it in rusty Polish,

and it was more musical than I ever thought Polish
could be. She grew large as she spoke,
she took it all in, let none of it out. Ah, mother,
you aren't the only godforsaken person here. It
isn't natural for such worries, for someone
to keep looking for omens. Your face is cardinal

red and your Polish nose is running. This time it
is beyond our speaking, how someone
gets caught—motherless, in a wake of cardinals.

When the lilacs
exploded in May, there wasn't much else to do
but take in the scent. Iowa: before

the skies opened and poured enough rain to coat
the grass with slick mushrooms, the pavement
with worms.
            I'd drive on gravel roads away from the river.
Barns crooked, splintering. The corn stunted and slow
to leaf. An expanse of fields, a slanted
mailbox, makeshift fence.
                The gypsum mines were lit
up at night, the air flour-white. Workers
underground in machines big enough to take down

a house. An endless circuit of tunnels, alarms connected
to the ventilation system, and planned escape
        routes. I mapped the region, knew

the slight rises and sudden drops that even flatness
could afford. I knew all the ways to leave—the bridge
rusting in its piles.
          That spring, the lilacs were too early,
the neighbor's mare foaled a spotted colt. In the brown

Mississippi, a teenager was still trapped in a red truck,
and a sleepwalker dreamt he was in a race and was
      crushed by a semi. One suicide, then two
impersonators. What I can't shake off—
                  tremors underfoot
caused by weapons testing at the military base, fist-sized
geodes, the historic library with glass floors
        earthquake-cracked, the glint

of a man's gold watch face. Eyes of deer

along the highway, orange pearls, stone
ghost-figures in morning fog.

I've placed a rock at the base of my bed.
I pray if you come back
                    this will keep you out.

The barn's roof under frost
      consolidates the landscape's impassive
      guise. The grasses have retreated
         into a hardened form. Notable days: blue
      sky, a sailor's twilight, clouds extinguishing

the town. I've seen what was here and what was
      yet to come. The paper mill destroyed by fire,
      a buffalo head over a tavern door, the gun
         factory roosting on its cliff of lead. Black
      and white prints in archives, boxes filled

with negatives. The Hungarian curator knows each
      building by its bricks, time of day by sun-glare
      on windows, direction by thicker branches
         on a tree's side. I could spend years investigating
      what was never mine. Alleyways

and smokehouses, wrought-faced workers stowing salt
      onto trains. A young woman in an Easter bonnet, posed
      on a porch step, snow at her feet. By now the sheets
         have been brushed down, straightened, the house
      put in order. It's her expression that gets me—her ink-

circled eyes, lips chewed. Before the camera she's textless,
      reticent as all portraits become. Lives we invent
      to catalogue our own misgivings. I'm no expert.
         The woman doesn't want to go back inside. I'm in
      the kitchen cleaning a fish. Rain hasn't come yet, but it will.

Hardly there anymore, a silhouette
guards the inlet. Manitou Islands
obscured by sand, trees

match-sticked. We trolled
        for Petoskey stones, found one
among the motley

pebbles, immersed in fluvial
deposits, rough bottom, emergence. Consider
        the water, once warmer—coral

colonies feeding on plankton, its tissue
        cemented into a honeycomb.
Sediment-grouted, petrified—

It's humbling
what happens to flesh. In myth,
        transfiguration seems more

painful—the permanence of it—
maddened nightingale, gnarled
        laurel, sleeping bear.

To know release—your own

dissolve. A commissure—your body into
        mine, the slip
of being here and elsewhere. You are

not you any longer. The dunes
        shift, restructure their crescents,
each particle undone.

Paintings in waiting
rooms accentuate the
appalling décor

of teal plastic
chairs, confetti
carpet, and the homey

wallpaper dappled with
a rosette motif.
Whoever felt

inclined to place
baskets of silk
pink flowers on

each window-
sill hasn't been
moved to dust

them. Smudges on the
pane, a housefly.
The paintings are

the same—either
architectural shapes:
looming triangle,

halved circle. Or the
landscape in calm
relief. Trees edged

with winter, white-blue
snow swept
nothingness. Toneless

sky. The subject
backing
away from itself.

The hands give it away—hard-felt,
                carried in fistfuls. Pins or jaggedness, or

there's always something—as in
              happening, going, about to

go wrong. If there's a way out, it's through
            the dirt—as in in it, underneath
        the nails, nervous grit of the brain, rooted.

: : :

Holding it, there was a guilt-
                  look, sideways. Perhaps in the tilt

     of the head, shoulders exposed,
              the weirdly blushed
         hesitation worn before

              answering. Or that by looking in
      the mirror could answer for you.

: : :

It's the shop that makes you
              feel good, being there
     in the middle of all the new, untouched

        merchandise. As if what comes
     and goes will forever be
         this way—needing broken in.

: : :

After a while, the steps had to be done
            a particular way—hushed, kept

    in check. So even a phone call
            became a test, a removal from

        what the soul wished for. No redress,
                        not any one clue.

: : :

Disappointment comes dandied up in your Sunday
            best. Stockings bunched
                at the knees, patent shoes buckled, smart—

    a teacherly click click on the tile. Not
                that it could be avoided, not that you had
        anything to do with it.

: : :

When the hands lock into
            fists, the skin pays—

    tautness to slack, loss of
            restraint. As if the excess could

        be wrung out, replaced by
    another another. Vigilant.

                You weren't left
                    with much better.

It was a matter of untangling: I'd be the one to undo
knots in hair or thread   or rub off the price
tag on gifts. Anything   my fingers could get
into and tear apart.   It was task-to-complete; it was
a clean surface that counted, each   wrinkle pressed and corners
tucked. You would   fold down sheets
or winter things for   storage. They'd never fit;
the woolens refusing to stay   flat, the chest over-packed.
Your weight on it, sister-   with-a-broken-heart. First
resistance,   then give.

Covered—the first
of winter edges forward, unmistakably

fixed—the man in the cemetery, worn
as the historical slate

markers, stood back
to the wind. With the coal companies, quality-side

Cornwall, Pennsylvania—I don't know why we
lived there. I'm from

a family of coal-, steel-workers myself. It was rot—
needles and damp

leaves—gave the place a down-home smell. Went down
in four-hundred foot mines every

Friday. *Come see the places where I doo lie.* Brazil, Canada—I was
good at sniffing out the good

stuff. Poles, Slovaks, Italians persuaded—*As you are
now once was I*—to work. Would bear their own

bad tidings—black lung, alcoholism, layoffs. Union would
strike and they'd walk the

line Thanksgiving to New
Years. No oranges in any shoes Saint Nicholas Day. Saint

Casimir's empty. I'm not bitter. *As I am now soon
you must be.* I know it—Johnstown, place

that floods, flooded. Whole pumpkin field one
fall, swept by Stonycreek

River, bobbed the channel and rats pushed out in
downtown streets. Good

Samaritan Hospital—woman in wheelchair cries Lordy,
Lordy Almighty. *Prepare yourself*

to follow me. This isn't there—
it's upstate New York and he's telling me his

mother called him Dick—no mistake. Town's
not the only burnt

coaltown—Centralia, Shamokin.
All the companies got quality guys wheedling

production efficiency, gross profits. Tell those
numbers (over 2,209) to the burning

pockets of steel tycoons—lost their resort, reservoir.
Got record snow-melt, rain that

season—dam burst and it went
with force enough to carry a 48-ton locomotive.

Stone Bridge didn't budge, held the debris, caught
fire. Inextinguishable,

dumb rotten luck. Been there?—lovely
place. Haven't been there

in ages. People aged forty-two, sixteen lying under us—
spring deaths, not winter,

or maybe it did them in.

The valley's blue and steely-snow was a relief

to the eyes. To those workers in mine-black
soot, who slugged away at the veins,
                                    and deeper still,
hit gas pockets or water, the job was better
than nothing at all.

: : :

Something's hit anyway,
                        fortune-craze, up hard.
Because one body was expected to do the work
of ten, and every one needed

to get ahead. Boys skinny as goats sent in
the narrowest cracks,
                        forget the canaries
that died. Many
tangled, knees to chest, if lucky,

got pulled out later once noticed missing.

: : :

After the mines, it was the blast furnace, the pig
iron's liquid orange—devil's pit,
                            end-all.
Faces bronzed, cracked,
early-aged. Relief was not a part of it,
                        though the valley's snow

and steely-blue relieved the eyes, but then how
do I know?
                    I was a stray American. The metallurgical
plants were all that were hiring. Bethlehem Steel, Appalachian

coal mines, or the Gary factories. No one had much

: : :

choice. In what we learned
                    it was mostly invention
of the coke ovens, difference between bituminous

and anthracite—the dollars
of industry. Never steel fabrication, accident
                                        or accident,

strikes, Molly Maguires, slow burn. The ruinous
conclusion of land after strip—
                    slag, the shoddy heap

of refineries, sludge, toxic runoff. Never
the what-to-do-with-it-after.

: : :

For all the engineering feats and safety
measures, it was the snow

        that consoled our blue-steeled eyes.

Some sight. The skin nettled by winter's
clench, the outlying hills filling in

white. Steam pit, wholesale

consumption, jackpot, laughing stock—
moles, blacked, of the earth.

: : :

Under ground, I am mineral, I am
ghost. The mine shaft's walls glint

silver. My heart is in my ear, I am
headlamp shine to see.

All insides, all pit.

I'd say what is golden is green for each season,
the various blooms perfuming, sticking heavily
to their stalks. No place could be so
overbooked with charm the water runs
from the mountains straight into a flock
of hills clouds overhang all day or the breeze
in cool rolls from the ocean summer evaporated
into mist as here. Paradise: the trees resistant
more than anything, limbs twisted
willowy, the bark colorized by the sun's all-touching
watch. The dry-hazed grass vulnerable to spark
the whole slope off. What thoughts
don't bend toward disaster will instead the earth
to stay in place, as one hopes flames or offense will
pass by. A difficulty to dwell in: the valley's
splendor has commissioned rest, canonized
hilltop to hilltop, delicate space—a pause.

You'd think I have no conviction

going back   and forth like this.
Some hunger is all—the ribs bowed

and stacked. It was the only way
I could get anywhere: taking

what was offered.   None of it
gratitude, none of it filled me.

Until this absence turned into

an exquisite thing   like the formation of
the cosmos, imploding on its own

vacuity.   Or as in
smallness, mistakes: the robin's dud egg—

the *what-could-have-been* I am still finding.

A field of sorts, fucked over
by flower: shepherd's purse, cocklebur cordate

and hooked. A rather haphazard collection it is,
cordoned by wire, massed in clump

the greenbrier, the clover rooted and reaching
up from the in-between spaces, as any

thing green and erratic, as any meaning forced
into word or letter. A used place: a playground

or a dump of process, nutrients from decay,
bird droppings turned into seedlings, and

wind in the grass that opens the feeling of what is
unexamined. A permission taken for granted,

this field that is all-thought thought ungoverned.
It is the trespass that forms the to be.

Who knew—it's a riot of color each morning,
a pixelled play of opalesced grandeur
keeping clock in the cellular processes, tying
the abstract to the organic. Economical, salubrious
as all get-out a body washed in this type
of solar attention holds a piece of the celestial
earthbound. Call it a keepsake I've

been known to refuse. This earth's all
molten fire underneath, all threat
of extinction above. Last month, the ink-dipped
finger was the rage, today is about results
such as controlling the purple loosestrife
that's invaded northern marshlands.
I've put myself on the radar

as a conglomerate of affections,
overloaded, charged aurally, somewhat
vain or solipsistic like the Top 40 hits
"Live Like You Were Dying" and "Let Me
Love You." Intimacy's nice but a little
interlude is better. Who knew? Tedium's
in the grind, in sameness. So much so

that the coupling of nearly identical
specimens brings out the recessive
genes (i.e., deafness, albinoism). I'd rather
my spectral nature be showing, specious
as it is, vowel-coded, filled in color-by-number
with pencils that were once a rainforest.

This March, I'll go lamb-like
through the allergenic meadow, pass the sun-
crazed tubers pushing skyward. The horizon,
freckled with effects, will be coated a metallic
sheen. I'll be blasé with the season's fashionable
expression. I'll raise some dust as a fly.

Nickel-gray or computer
    consoled, not white or
        a failure as one might think
    when it appears on the return
mailing address label sent

    by the African Wildlife
        Foundation, which urges: "Spread
    the word about the peril."
(Dense plantings of shrubbery
    provide safe areas.) Too

        large an idol to hide from
    the rest, it takes residence
in one's brain as the serene
    center aimed for in classical
        Hindu meditation. Several lifetimes

    are required to untangle
the self. Said to inhabit
    certain remarkable capacities
        (such as insensitivity to heat
    or cold, and though ears are key

to ventilation, passage
    through the Pyrenees
        is not an option) it walks
    noiselessly despite bulk. A dutiful
mourner with its own funeral

    march, herds fifteen to thirty
        can't bring back the mammoth,
    though several in Siberia were
found wholly preserved
    in ice. The fashion now is

to save, use the ground
tusk powder only in dire
situations. Ticks, as the red-billed
oxpecker suggests, can
bring down a good dog

though not when the bird is perched
on the elephant's high back. Just as,
to boost a career,
having one sit on one's
desk is good luck.

All the great artists were designing curtains
        for the Unemployment Department
in Moscow. Mayakovsky coined the words
                for the pacifier advertisement that shows
        torpedoes whizzing into a baby's round mouth.

        The caption reads: "In transforming nature, man
transforms himself," under a photograph of an emaciated
                labor camp prisoner in Gorky's Belomar project.
        Realism was just what the authorities wanted.
These were beautiful times. After the War, after

the purges,
        Eisenstein was condemned for his film
where Ivan the Terrible acted as a stand-in
        for Stalin. Symphonies tumbled
into dissonance.
                What's that Fadeyev? You
say you are guarding a latrine? Zoshchenko's
monkey was truthful; Anna Akmatova's love
        poetry was too decadent, too bourgeois.
Brodsky was a parasite, Bulgakov long dead
                by the time the devil took grip in Moscow.

        Before all this, Malevich was busy designing
what would be "The New Form of Art."
        His painting "The Black Square" tells us:
whatever you can build with your mind
can order reality.
                Easily reproducible, it stands
solidly, a weight behind your eyelids. A square
because it's functional, highly modern. Black
        and unobtrusive, so you will not be
                impressed by where it's all leading.

This is no vacation. Breakfast
made us sick, maybe some air
will do us good. We'll walk
to the Ob Sea, but it's not

really a sea, just a dammed river
where little yellow birds fly
in a circle and a circle
and never land. In Borovöe

nothing is easy. The mosquitoes
are murder. The phone is dead
the bored receptionist insists
and then it rings. The doctor shuffles

in his office. Behind locked doors
there are machines that help
the students breathe.
Nobody told us the Russian

word for resort is sanatorium. They say,
you should relax, we have a hydro-
electric bath, we say *nyet spasibo*.
How much does a place

affect a person? These kids
are from a city not marked
on any map, where uranium
and premature babies are made.

Where Kan River means Blood
River, the water laced with iron,
the soil and air as bad. But the songs
the girls sing about the cold and lost

husbands, about dead horses
make you forget your complaints. At dinner,
I say, no soup for me
please, move your elbows. Comrade,

are you going to *eat* that meat?
From the dark kitchen, the nurse
carries off a tray with food
samples sealed in

sterilized test tubes. Look
how wonderfully the light
plays off that cucumber!
Oh, how the mind can fool

you! Haven't we had enough
for today? We should rest
a while. We'll take the night
off, go to the *banya*, take a dip

in the pool. Together
we'll sit in a steaming closet
and later, to improve our health
we'll beat each other with sticks.

Not so much for loosening as a geyser
to bottle. Hyper slug sheltered in the teeth's
horseshoe, silvery minefield. Consider the hurt
involved: piercings or lashings
dished out, the occasional bull or breeze
shot off. Not all talk is charmed: this one idiotic,
this one cheap, this one unfit for children (the cat,
the tie, the twister). With emphasis on zipping
or socking it, any one unleashed could be more
dangerous than a rabid dog. A little nip
of the bottle can warm the muscle, pardon
the slip, Frenchify the smooch. Ah, the ecstasy
involved! The buds aroused and salivating!
Some flame, some groove, the very tip
sharpened. Annunciate that again, won't you,
dear? Serpent-slick, tricky: knot the cherry
stem, touch nose, or spin a yarn as it's bound
to do. Potty mouth, how will you sweet
yourself out this time? Lozenge the organ, rest
the pipes. The cut won't sting if the air's kept clean.
A yawn, a clearing: let it be swallow or exhaust.

Mary, where do you lay yourself down, when do you
give it a rest? Holy, holy, holy and there's no donkey

for you anymore, all draped in sheets, left iconic
on the kitchen wall. Girl-wife, teen-mother. The lover

of infinitude, hot heaven's breath. Figure me for a goner,
repentant, noncommittal, spotting your face in the Windex-

washed skyscraper, the metallic oil swirl as headlined
in the tabloids. Apparition Mary in Egypt, six pigeons

in tow, televised, and pope-approved. Typhoid of roses,
fuchsia-lipped (our Lady's eardrop), white-waxy face

and a kindness I could never. Starlet dove. Known
to be found in an agate rock cracked open, your image

is nature-written and fortified. Choice of firstfruits, tree
of good foliage, the white-spotted thistle leaves spotted so

from drops of your breast milk. Cultish from your first
elongated neck and plaintive posture over the unearthly

baby. As if maternity could tell the end all, the divine
delivered from a common uterus, womanly

restraint. Garden enclosed. Pearly matron, blesséd without
question. Mary in disguise, Mary the lucrative

commodity. Epithetic Mary, where is your comforting?
Your appearance means salvation for the fiery girls you approach

on cliff rock and extend your heart bearing sorrows
to. Impossible coincidence, burden

upon burden to preserve your virginity, veiled
maidenhead. The Lord's been with you and how

it's plagued the clergy's imagination, that physical
union. Priestly rod blossoming without root. Birth

without pain, materialized passion, vine bearing
grapes. Mary ensconced in grotto, lily among the thorns,

woman who opens, woman assembled by many
names, medium through which miracle performs its cameo.

Fool with her enough and she'll unspool,

each wound roll uncurled, snagged and ink-
pooled at the sentence's end. Cue up the hush

> (You'd nest in
> that room, too,
> with a winter so
> enduring.)

words, the lagging bits that need more
explication. Bring out

the dictionary. A fumbling
with lock and key—finger ballet,

> (She'll come apart
> —*cut the twine.*)

sweeping over the weave. Braille-coded,
and the brain's own coils

> (There's no polite
> way to put this.
>
> —*Say it.*
>
> You'd muck her up.)

surrounding the riddle. Fame, not fear,
was the impulse. A saintly

version of wife. Pet bird. Because one

can't be tied down

(She'll wind upward
—*called back.*)

in a devotion without its quirks.
Because it's enough

(Divinity.

—*Right.*)

to mix the self up in it. Emily in
white, Emily in her own.

Because you never said *heal,* because

she healed too easily. You
held it in, plotted

the snubs in her garden—misgivings all
in a row. Because she put them on

the shelf, you scrutinized
the china, her gestures.

You are so brittle the way you tug

at your hands and thin
yourself out. Because you weren't

there, she stitched herself
a scarf for winter, purled

unevenly—dropped the slip.

You took it anyway,
she never said *don't.*

Take the concentration intricate
work requires—a needle, embroidery. The in

and out through the eye, thread and
fabric pulled. Or the cautious

hands of my mother, webbing yarn
into a sweater, the genius

click of her needles. It's enough
to make me jealous of that kind

of patience. When I took the box of give-
away stuff to the garage

I found swatches of crepe and a lace
tablecloth discolored by

wine, as if a dinner party had
decided to throw their bad manners out

in the open, leave their spoils. The luxury
of this fabric, its airy matter.

I'd like to tailor it, get it down
in a form myself. *All you need*

is a pattern, she'd tell me. No,
I thought, pawing my scissors,

one snag is all it takes,
one disruption—

It is not enough to keep the town pretty
       absolute or garment-like. The drift

shapes the afternoon into an ultrasilent room
       of covered things—throws

over furniture in the second house seaside.
       Windex-blue sky. The beach

swept of its soft sea bodies and the hard
       remains: Corrugated Jewel Box, Greedy

Dove. Sand dollars still pink and multi-legged, sun-
       bleached, final. I mean, it's boiling there

in the Mid-Atlantic Ridge—volcanic burblings
       and the sea floor shrinking as much as it is

expanding. All shift measured by echo, by
       millimeter. Unheard of. From where

you are you cannot stop the boat from
       moving across the water. Knowing no,

desperate. As if there's storm out
       there, the light gone all sick, green.

Wind marked across the dunes—graphic
       topography. Sundown red,

abstract, the way you like because it's easy
       to believe. As if movement

from knowledge to faith was that
       easy. Beyond, for good.

DEDUCTION

This is the work that was meant for us.
Drawn tight. Faces that give little
away. No more raising of eyebrows, no
more side-wary glances. As though silence
meant *to stuff down*. We trudged through
without complaint, gave the town a name and off
with the bankers' heads. What spills has been spilt
before. Who am I in this? Self-appointed scribe,
water-ring furthest from center. Doesn't matter,
everything was left as found. As if the foot
weren't a means out, composed of as many bones
as it is. I'd set out of here, but I'll admit, I like the view.

First, there were the broken pieces.
You said, don't you think I know

what I'm doing? To which I replied,
don't you feel most alone when we're in

this together? Under the eave, wasps
are constructing a nest, gray paper

out of spit, so much of the body
is in their work. See how

the legs move, bending and praying.
You said, don't you think I know

when you're trying to change the subject?
I could make a building out of my despair.

We could acquire a nice piece of land
and sit on it. There are a thousand blades

of grass, each one waiting
to be claimed. As I always say,

you said, if you commit one sin, then
you commit them all. To which I said,

how many absolutes do we have proof
of? The sky has never looked bluer.

What is the significance of that?
It means I might walk out on you

yet. What, you asked. Nothing,
I said, I said nothing. What is there

to say anyway, except in the sunlight,
I could see the glass fall even before

your elbow knocked it over.
This is always how it happens, certain

ideas are never fully formed.
This is some mess, you said.

To which I said, there are lives
that go on this way. Then we went

down on our knees, and
in that manner, we began.

"Clearing the Yard": Italicized line from Dostoevsky's *The Brother Karamazov*, Pevear and Volokhonsky's translation.

"What's Discovered Is Wiped Out": "Sympathies: the windy sky parts now in flocks" belongs to Susan Wheeler from her poem "Farmers, Falling Down" in *Bag 'o' Diamonds*.

"Wave Factor": Local lore in the Finger Lakes Region in upstate New York claims that Cayuga and Seneca Lake, the deepest two lakes, contain layers of warmer and colder water which often trap drowned bodies in the convection current.

"Any Good Scientist Could Tell You": "All human errors are impatience, a premature breaking off of methodical procedure, an apparent fencing-in of what is apparently at issue," Franz Kafka.

"Tongues Of": Concerning ecstasy, St. Teresa of Ávila wrote, "O my God, what must a soul be like when it is in this state! It longs to be all one tongue with which to praise the Lord."

"The Toy Divine(s)": "The toy divines the invisible substance of things," Daniel Tiffany's *Toy Medium: Materialism and Modern Lyric*. "One was so busy keeping you alive that no one had time to determine what you were," taken from Rilke's essay, "On the Wax Dolls of Lotte Pritzel."

"Three Constructions": Based on Joseph Cornell constructions.

"Lives of Astrologers" is for Elaine Bough.

"A Sorry Concept, That Town": "Came the yellow days of winter, filled with boredom" from Bruno Schultz's "Birds," in *The Street of Crocodiles*.

"Dzien Dobry": Polish for "good day."

"In the Land of Sleeping People": According to the *Dictionary of Place Name Derivations*, "Iowa" is the French form of a Sioux word signifying the drowsy or the sleepy ones.

"Pall": Italicized lines are from a gravestone outside Trumansburg, New York: "Eunice Tracy and her child. Wife of Arza Tracy. Eunice Tracy departed this life April the 25th the year 1815 and in the 42nd year of her age. And her child died April the 12th 1815." Facts about the 1889 Johnstown, Pennsylvania flood are from Richard O'Connor's *Johnstown: The Day the Dam Broke*.

"Telluric": "I was a stray American" from John Scott's *Behind the Urals*.

"Sanctuary": After A. R. Ammons.

"An Opening Onto": After Robert Duncan.

"Spectrum": "The fly sat upon the axel-tree of the chariot-wheel and said, 'What a dust do I raise!'" Aesop, *Fables*, "The Fly on the Wheel."

"Our Lady of Appearances": "Mary, mother of us, where is your comforting?" from Hopkins's "No worst there is none. Pitched past pitch of grief."

"Blind Feel": "Called back" is Dickinson's epitaph.

"Measures": "From where you are you cannot stop the boat from moving across the water" is derived from a Zen Buddhist koan.

1987
   Elton Glaser, *Tropical Depressions*
   Michael Pettit, *Cardinal Points*
1988
   Bill Knott, *Outremer*
   Mary Ruefle, *The Adamant*
1989
   Conrad Hilberry, *Sorting the Smoke*
   Terese Svoboda, *Laughing Africa*
1990
   Philip Dacey, *Night Shift at the Crucifix Factory*
   Lynda Hull, *Star Ledger*
1991
   Greg Pape, *Sunflower Facing the Sun*
   Walter Pavlich, *Running near the End of the World*
1992
   Lola Haskins, *Hunger*
   Katherine Soniat, *A Shared Life*
1993
   Tom Andrews, *The Hemophiliac's Motorcycle*
   Michael Heffernan, *Love's Answer*
   John Wood, *In Primary Light*
1994
   James McKean, *Tree of Heaven*
   Bin Ramke, *Massacre of the Innocents*
   Ed Roberson, *Voices Cast Out to Talk Us In*
1995
   Ralph Burns, *Swamp Candles*
   Maureen Seaton, *Furious Cooking*
1996
   Pamela Alexander, *Inland*
   Gary Gildner, *The Bunker in the Parsley Fields*
   John Wood, *The Gates of the Elect Kingdom*

1997
   Brendan Galvin, *Hotel Malabar*
   Leslie Ullman, *Slow Work through Sand*
1998
   Kathleen Peirce, *The Oval Hour*
   Bin Ramke, *Wake*
   Cole Swensen, *Try*
1999
   Larissa Szporluk, *Isolato*
   Liz Waldner, *A Point Is That Which Has No Part*
2000
   Mary Leader, *The Penultimate Suitor*
2001
   Joanna Goodman, *Trace of One*
   Karen Volkman, *Spar*
2002
   Lesle Lewis, *Small Boat*
   Peter Jay Shippy, *Thieves' Latin*
2003
   Michele Glazer, *Aggregate of Disturbances*
   Dainis Hazners, *(some of) The Adventures of Carlyle, My Imaginary Friend*
2004
   Megan Johnson, *The Waiting*
   Susan Wheeler, *Ledger*
2005
   Emily Rosko, *Raw Goods Inventory*
   Joshua Marie Wilkinson, *Lug Your Careless Body out of the Careful Dusk*